ISBN-13: 978-1-956775-21-1

LCCN: 2022906745

Table of Contents

Introduction

Living in a time when we deal with various diseases and viruses almost daily, health is an issue. That is an understatement. Could our health be yet another reason we also find ourselves in needless debates over what is of God and what is not of God? The daily serving of communicated perspectives on the beast's mark and what is not is almost mind boggling.

There have been far too many opinions concerning medical treatments for these same viruses and diseases, and we still see people dying. The prophet of today knows that in our assignments, we will run into many different types of people.

Some of these people will be sick with various types of ailments, and a prophet is an option that people depend on to deliver the will of God in whatever manner God dictates through His servants. I dare to ask, "Are we well ourselves?"

There is a divine connection between the soul of a prophet and their health. We must learn, practice, and teach the divine connection between the soul and our health. We are called to help others, but we need to help ourselves in the process. 3 John 1:2 says 'Beloved,' which means us.

God is clear that above all things that we prosper and be in health, even as our soul prospereth. There is a reality that 3 John 1:2 gives us great insight that we may have overlooked.

The results of what I discuss in this book about the soul will not come overnight. This is a commitment to do the needed and necessary work. We, the prophets, need to do this for our health.

Do not fool yourself; there is no magical formula here, just prophets doing the work we need to do to grow and be better for God's creation. Let me also state that I have become the first partaker; join me as we now live in divine health.

CHAPTER 1

What Prophets Don't Consider About Our Health

Our proposed overlooking has cost us greatly. Let's quickly establish that I am not a medical physician, so I offer no medical advice, but I believe in God's Word.

I am a prophet, as many of you are, and I realize the need to look deeper like many of you. Prophet let's look at the Word of God, and find some insight on our souls in relationship to our health.

Let's begin with a question? What position are our souls in? Do we know? Do we care? Can we say? Psalms 23 says He restores my soul. There are some places we can't go and some things God can't do for us unless He restores our souls.

Health is a critical issue in our lives. We need God on this journey. God has what we need, which is the key to accessing divine health. Prophet, if there ever was a time to have good health, it is now!

Let's identify a fact. The soul is the computer that operates within us. It is our indicator that works between the spirit and the body. The soul is that part of us critical to our thinking and communication with God.

We are doing ourselves a great disservice when we ignore our health and the soul's part in it. This is why this message is being given to you. God has something for us to learn and practice, so let's explore this issue.

My assignment here is to open your mind to the realm of knowing and learning something about ourselves that maybe we did not realize. Let me also say that we can't allow our lack of soul prosperity to no longer hinder our health.

Today's enemy is coming at us with literally everything and many things that we may not be aware of. We have a responsibility to position and fulfill the promises of God.

We, the now generation prophets, are the mouthpieces of God. Prophet, our health is a kingdom reality promised in God's Word. Let us familiarize ourselves with this fact. This season, we are subject to our health and the forces capable of harming us. We must realize this season is a season we will regret if we do not take care of ourselves. This is the time. We must now, more than ever, take care of ourselves.

I will not remind you of the pandemic. We all have our stories about it, and its residue still lingers and probably will. My question is, how many people have we lost when we may not have had to? Could our lack of understanding of the relationship between our health and our soul cost us as prophets?

God's healing power is available for all of us as prophets. I can't stress enough how vital our soul is to our health. The very release of our excellent general health awaits us as we develop ourselves in the Word of God.

This book will afford you the ability to explore the revelation of the soul and your health. We must be able to fulfill the work of God for the kingdom of God.

Prophets, let us look at ourselves first. This has to be our first step. We desire to be healed physically, yet the process involves more than

that. There are spiritual and mental considerations that we need to consider.

These considerations are critical and priceless
not just to us but also to those sent to minister.
Our responsibility is what it is, and we must be
ready.

The title of this chapter speaks to what we
have not considered about our health because we
are anointed. We need to be the first partakers of
God's plan for divine health.

Like many of you, I have been bombarded with
this herbal product and that all-natural product.
I can attest to the products I have tried, but I
can't overlook God's solution for my health.

We can believe and still not process information correctly and block our healing. No prophet,
not a single one of us in our right mind, would
want to block our healing, but let's consider the
fact that maybe we have. This is a real possibility.

What's in our life that is not of God, maybe
even satanic? Where is it at? The one place in us

it can only be is our soul. Think about the fact that the enemy cannot invade your spirit and that your body must be fed.

The only acceptable and available place to the enemy is our soul. This is the opening for demonic forces and the trouble they bring to our lives. Remember that the soul is the human-computer for us. The soul communicates with the Holy Spirit and feeds our mind and body.

We should accept that God can deal with our ailments as He knows everything. We know that and realize that God teaches and prepares us through our experiences, especially our troubles and struggles. We need to learn more about the supernatural relationship between our soul and our health.

When not correctly adhered to, our health is full of trouble and struggles for us. So let's ask the question, where is God in all this? He is everywhere simultaneously, and yes, He is in the midst of what is going on in our souls.

Can we trust God with what we are dealing with in our thinking towards our ailments? I submit that we have overlooked the very fact, costing us dearly.

This means that our thoughts are not in the God word processing mode. Our thoughts are in the physical model, stopping the pain and letting me feel better.

God has given us a divine right to healing, and the reality, prophet, is that we need to change our thinking. I so wish I could make you believe this with everything in you, but that is one thing you must do for yourself, prophet.

There is a reality that our good health is like new a new wine; it is necessary for the Body of Christ. It is essential for today's church. The scripture says that no man should put his old wine in a new bottle. New wine should go in new bottles.

Luke 5:37 says new wine must be in new bottles or the old bottle will burst and spill. The keyword is spill. Prophet, we can't afford to get information from God on our health, and we allow it to spill.

We do this by allowing ourselves to ignore and pay the information no mind. Dismiss the spirit of ignore in your life. Please do yourself a favor and dismiss this dangerous spirit from your life.

The Body of Christ as a whole has a habit of us ignoring each other. Various faiths will ignore each other and various gifts like the prophetic, we will ignore each other. Again you would be wise to dismiss this spirit from your life, especially as we speak about divine health.

We "spill" information when we ignore it. That is a total waste. We can't allow ourselves to waste information. Prophets, the soul relationship, and the soul status are more profound and meaningful than many realize.

The soul's key to our health is critical. My goal and desire for you are to help you activate your soul's prosperity through your health. This means that your health is going to be in a better place.

This means that you will be healthy and affect others as God sends you to the nations. Men and women have died in this season, which is a part of life. How many have died because of poor or no interaction of the healing or activation of the soul?

Now prophet, look at the new bottle in Luke 5. Here is the new and improved divine health that we will walk in once we get the revelation of the soul's responsibility and trust our changed minds of the subject.

Do not put the new information in the old bottle. This is a biblical principle, and we know it will not work. The scripture is clear on that.

How many of us will admit the fact that we have spent much of our lives in the physical mode of thinking regarding our health? Are you willing to change your mind and get healthy?

We have kids, grandkids, and people who love and need us to be the prophets, seers, watchmen, and apostles of this generation, and that within itself is a big chore.

Recently I have changed my mind and my thinking on health. I have truly learned that my soul is critical in developing my overall health.

I plan and believe that my work for God will span generations, which means I need to be around for quite a while. So in light of that, I need to ensure that I am healthy. I am speaking Isaiah 58:8 upon my life daily, which reads "Then your light shall break forth like the morning, Your healing shall spring forth speedily, And your righteousness shall go before you; The glory of the LORD shall be your rear guard."

My soul is open to this word. I encourage each of you to read and digest this word for yourselves. This is part of the many important issues we must discuss.

The advent of issues like the Corona Virus has raised our attention to all-new levels of our health issues. Many of us may have been surprised; little did we see ourselves being quarantined for long periods and making adjustments in our lives.

We had to make adjustments, but our bodies still required certain things needed for divine health. This is why you are reading this book, prophet. Our health is part of our prophetic DNA, just like other specialists or professionals need to be aware of their gifting DNA.

God has reminded us that He still has a plan for our lives. He has the answers that we need to seek. We are to use the tools God has provided for us. The soul of a prophet is the point of attack. Prophets this has to be understood, and we have to be keenly aware of our souls' health.

It is a special part of the prophet's life. Everything revolves around the soul in their life. The importance of the prophet's soul can't be overstated. This is what makes our mentality such a huge issue. I submit a genuine concern that we have not paid enough attention to this very fact. We must submit our due diligence to the soul and its effect on health.

My prayer is that you will do what I did and change your mind on how you look at your health. Personally, when I look at my parents, I know I come from good genes, but for me to depend on that alone is crazy and not enough.

We must utilize that our soul was God designed for our divine health. We are promised this in God's Word (3 John 2) . This is the foundational promise that I will stand on daily as I now work to soar in divine health.

Let me submit that the life cycle itself will expose us to different types of diseases. We may get sick. We may have days we feel better than others, but maintaining our health is critical.

As Prophets, we observe people, some for various periods. We form perspectives that many times are nothing like we thought. We are flawed, and we would do well to realize that sometimes God will open our eyes to see the reality of who these people are.

You will see their issues, their problems, and yet something is still missing in your perspective.

You're asking yourself, "What is it?" Here now the submission to our learning must begin, and we understand on a different level than we have in the past.

We are the now generation seers; we are specialists who must constantly focus on our total development and health. Health is an area we must develop in. We can shout all night and not make any progress on our health.

Out thinking must be in the mode of development in this sense.   How can we help others? How can we be the exponent of God's work when we ourselves are broken, down, and too sick to execute His divine will? Together let's reconstruct our thinking about divine health. There is power in developing the soul, and let's discuss this and get it fixed.

How we perceive the situation is the key to how we get enlightened. Are you willing to change your perspective to get enlightened? Sometimes we realize the light too late, and we live in the valley of regret. Our goal has to be to do better. We have the opportunity to do better and live better.

Many prophets have been blindsided and today live in spiritual blindness about the soul's participation in their health. Prophets, your challenge is that God would give each of us "a spirit of wisdom and revelation in the true knowledge of Him."

To know these spiritual truths, God must open our eyes. Let me repeat this. We must restructure our thinking, especially in terms of the soul.

CHAPTER 2

Let's Restructure Our Thinking Prophet

There are four kinds of prophets in today's Gospel you can't help. No matter what you do or how hard you try, there are four kinds of prophets you can't help. These prophets will not change, nor will they restructure their thinking either.

1. You can't help a prophet who refuses to acknowledge or believe they have a problem.
2. You can't help a prophet who feels you are the problem.
3. You can't help a prophet who comes to you for direction, and they have a better solution than you do.
4. You can't help a prophet who rejects sound biblical principles based on the Word of God.

We have now established these four facts; let's now start restructuring our thinking process with Psalms 139:14, which says that "I will praise thee. For I am fearfully and wonderfully made: marvelous are thy works; and that my soul knoweth right well."

Let's look at the fact that this describes how God makes us. We need to alert ourselves to the other point that our "soul knoweth right well."

We are to keep ourselves aware of this very important fact. Sadly we may not teach on this enough, so let us now feed on this.

Let us take an inventory. How many of us can say that our soul knoweth right well? Look closely at what's spoken. We have complete and total health spoken to us in the Word of God. Prophets, we can't miss this.

We are moving in God's total health when our souls knoweth right well. I don't know about you, but I can only speak for myself. I know I want this because God has promised it to us and it is exciting.

Prophet, when people see healing, they want to ascend to a place or the state of the "soul knoweth right well" stage. Many times they are overwhelmed by emotions and excitement as they come. People are like kids wanting toys at Christmas. We should be the same way with the promises of God.

They see the work of God through the prophet or God's servant, and the work is taking a toll on our bodies. Does it seem like the anointing itself is beating us down, especially after we minister? This is very similar to Elijah after he performed various miracles (1 Kings 18), and later, he was totally empty.

Are we not strong enough in our bodies to maintain the anointing? The issue here is that the problem is in the soul, the human processing computer. I believe even the great Elijah experienced this.

There is no way that the enemy of God was happy with Elijah. He had embarrassed the false God followers, beat and killed over 400 prophets of Baal by himself, and he ran for an estimated 25 miles ahead of a chariot in bad weather. He is attacked in the only place the enemy could, which was his soul. He is a victim of being spiritually blindsided through his soul.

I will discuss more on this principle later. Prophet, you too will be attacked in your soul that will ruin your health.

How can we help God's people when we need help ourselves? Therefore, "The Soul knoweth well" is important as the soul seeks to operate in full activation. Can you see why this is important to us as seers? The soul must be activated properly for the knowledge and revelation of divine health to flow.

Let us realize that this is an area that prophets have traditionally been subject to spiritual blindness (2 Peter 1:9). Peter deems those who fail increasingly to exhibit diligence in pursuit of spiritual virtue as blind or nearsighted. In Revelation 3:17, the exalted Lord of the church views the lukewarm but haughty Laodicean church.

The church was described as wretched, pitiful, poor, blind, and naked. We can look at our souls the same way we describe the Laodicean church. We have to realize the soul and health connection.

Spiritual blindness, therefore, is an issue when we refer to our soul and physical health. This prophet refers to our inability to comprehend a spiritual truth, specifically our failure to recognize the plan of God. This is why we are and should always be in learning mode. Amos 3:7 says, "Surely, God does nothing unless He reveals His secrets to His servants, the prophets."

As prophets, it is vital to conduct all our operations in the witness of the Spirit of God, who works to counteract the cataracts of Satan and reveal God's truth. The reality is that we can be gifted and still suffer from spiritual blindness.

The connection with the soul and our health is undeniable, prophets. We have focused on our souls to understand the human communication system. Now, can we see that we must also focus on the fact that the soul is the key to our health.

Let's consider that when our emotions, imagination, thoughts, and memory are in harmony, we obtain the "soul knoweth well" status. We are healthy and promised health, according to 3 John 1:2. Every prophet should know this, and every prophet should strive to be an example of this.

Prophet, there is a reality. Our health is being stolen from our souls. This is the opening that we are affected by. Can you realize this? The soul is the key. Our bodies only act on what we feed them.

The revelation is thought-provoking and needs to be considered by each of us in the prophetic. Our soul is the place, then we must give serious consideration in the pursuit of divine health. Our lives depend on it.

In chapter 1, we discussed that we need to change our thinking. Let us now look at that fact and see that our thinking is critical as prophets in the execution of our callings.

The mental approach to prophetic ministry can't be overstated. Can you see why we are talking about the soul? Remember, the soul is composed of your emotions, will, and mind. Can you now see a new and vital role that your soul must now accept? This is our responsibility to be aware of this fact.

The soul processing can't be stated enough. Let's examine ourselves. Have you lost count of how many times have you complained about this and that ailment? How often have we spoken death to what was supposed to be life?

How often has our imagination run wild, and we allow negative thoughts to cloud and ruin our minds and relationships? How often have we failed to correct ourselves when we could see and hear what God was saying to us?

Your mind always seeks something concrete out of that, but there's nothing concrete about our true nature unless we can validate it in the Word of God. This is the spirit-consciousness of a prophet.

Remember Prophet, God is a Spirit, and we worship Him in spirit and truth. Your soul connects to the directives of the Spirit of God. The soul then prospers especially our health.

Our health must consider the soul as it will lead us through spirit-consciousness and produces our thoughts. Prophet, we will live from these thoughts through our soul; this includes our beliefs, ideas, imagination, and emotions.

They are always accurate to us. This is the reality a Prophet lives in, and our soul functions around.

We move into our calling through this initial state of Prophetic Awareness to Prophetic Presence. It is the essence of being. The essence of being is knowing, and that is a soul function. We are living souls.

Therefore, Prophet, what awakens us from our spiritual sleep is knowing the difference between pure awareness (knowing you have something from God) and what you are aware of, which is knowing you have something.

Most prophets struggle with this and remain confused, unclear, and have many questions. The learning of themselves when they enter prophetic awakening is a soul process. Understanding this process now helps us understand the promise and blessing of divine health.

We perceive two ways when we read spiritual literature. We understand intellectually and emotionally. Both create barriers in our understanding. Still, we must die to both of these as prophets. Our soul is critical as we must move in the fullness of what God has called us to be.

The prophetic awakening develops our prophetic mentality. The prophetic mentality is a state of constant growth. Do not fool yourself. We always have areas of growth as long as we live. Let's make sure it is a long time. We must take the needed steps.

Now that we know this, let's talk more about changing our thinking. Many prophets will always play respect of person, as who is the messenger and do they like that person or not? This is true when we want to know, did God say this or that?

A prophet understands this fact and moves forth. We know this to be true, and this has broken and hurt so many in the prophetic community.

This very fact has lent to the ongoing soap opera we experience in the prophetic community and the Body of Christ. My point is that we have to change our thinking, which will change us in every area including our health.

We can change the way we think; we can keep ourselves healthy. This is not to say we skip medical checkups because it has a place in our lives.

The reality is that we so often overlook the benefit of medical professionals. God has people in the medical field, just like He has you and me in the prophetic ministry. Realize that and respect that in the same manner; you expect to receive respect. God has His people everywhere, just like He has prophets.

Our way of thinking sometimes is flawed, and we must change it. This is necessary to help us live and serve God as He has called us. Prophet, take your mentality seriously. Take the function of the soul seriously.

Prophet, we can't have anything stolen from our souls anymore. Our soul is the key to our health, and this is something we should be able to pass on as we demonstrate it daily.

Have you considered what it means to prosper and be in good health as your soul prospers? The reality is that we want to be in a position where our soul "knoweth right well."

We as prophets have to start now to think not with our thoughts but with the mind of God. We can only accomplish this total soul submission. Can we consider that we have not made the personal mental adjustments needed to live in real soul prosperity?

In my book, The Soul of the Issachar Seer, we explored the vital work of the soul as being developed for servitude to God. We see that the Issachar Seer's soul was highly developed in prosperity and was able to be used by God.

The activation of soul prosperity was the key to becoming the best version of oneself. As we become the best person, we can see that we also become more profound and have the absolute right to expect divine health.

This is an excellent concept that should benefit each of us for the rest of our lives. Prophet, there is absolutely no price for the benefit of good health. This is a priceless benefit.

You are a prophet, and despite how anyone may feel about you, the reality is you have a right to be healthy. Say to yourself that you will be healthy. I made my mind up that I, for one, know that I need to do this as I embark on my most incredible days ahead in servitude to God. Do you think that you need to do this?

As I speak prophetically to myself, Prophets, now speak prophetically to yourself and your health. Let me repeat this, you have a right to be healthy, and we need to know as much about it as possible.

Prophets, let us right now not only speak it but embrace it. Allow the past to be the past and what is behind you to stay there. We must focus our minds and thoughts on the right now!

We serve a right now God and are the mouthpieces of God. We are trusted to represent Him. Our being at our best is the very show of reverence and respect that we owe to God as His prophets.

The soul, the human computer or laptop has to function properly for you to function correctly here on the earth. Can you think of how important it is to prosper and be in good health? Let me stress again. This is God's Word.

There is a reality that my soul must prosper as my entire being is connected to it. This includes my function as a prophet. This is a fact that no prophet can know and ignore.

Where is God sending you the prophet? What is the message He wants you to bring? How are you to complete your assignment when your health is not working in divine order as it is designed?

The world gives us diets, fads, pills, and even daily theories about our health. Prophet, are we to ignore what God is saying about our health? Should we trust the wisdom of the world and not believe the Word of God? That would be an insult to God, and because you are a prophet, that takes it to a whole new degree.

There cannot be a thought that God would not equip His divinely called servants and not give them all the tools they need, especially for divine health. God is not sending us out ill-prepared and not knowing. Prophet, when we know better, we must do better.

Prophet, "my soul, knoweth well." "I will praise thee; for I am fearfully and wonderfully made. Speak to God about what He says about you. Say that marvelous are thy works and that my soul knoweth right well." Can you proclaim that fact? Will you speak that prophet with the belief that you are all in?

The very ability we need to speak this is that we stand on His Word, and our faith is moving to another place where it has not been.

Can you stand to be empowered by God through His Word? This is the same word that you speak into your lives, and it should be good enough to speak into your life.

Under no circumstances should we, as prophets, allow our souls to be robbed by the enemy into making us think that negative thoughts about our health are good or benefit us. Speak to yourself and say that you will not let your emotions, imagination, thoughts, or memory dictate how you see your health.

Now that you know you are wonderfully made as part of God's marvelous works, your mind and thoughts must change. You are made in His image, and your soul is critical to practicing these thoughts and insight. Now we need to focus more on the soul to activate it into the place of soul prosperity.

We will find that we are at the place where we must realize what our soul is capable of. This is God showing and teaching us how to take control of our health and be effective in our servanthood. He has given us the key, and we now must take control, use, and monitor our souls.

What is attempting to rob me? What is empowering me? We have identified the area of concern that we must be aware of. Let us now utilize what we know and make it work, prophet. It is soul activation time.

CHAPTER 3

Prophet Activate Your Soul For Your Health

Let us now look at Psalms 103 as we renew and remind our souls that we belong to God. Our souls must be submitted to God. David has the key. He adequately says to himself to, "Bless the Lord oh my soul and all that is in me." Notice closely what David says.

He tells his soul to bless God. Look closely at verse one, and it will jump out at you. We are talking about the kingdom health that dominates sickness, and as we examine, we see the keywords. Bless the Lord, oh my soul. Say it again over and over as it gets in your spirit.

"Bless the Lord, oh my soul." We all pray but do we all tell our souls to bless God as David demonstrates to us. Are we willing to submit to this? As prophets and mouthpieces of God, do we understand what David teaches us in this example?

David is demonstrating what it means to take authority over your soul. How many of us are doing various things that block us from total health? Have we taken authority over our soul?

I said earlier that I wish I could do this for you, but I pray that you will discover it. This is a full-time endeavor for me to do my due diligence as it will be for you also, my prophetic peer.

We must command our soul (emotions, mind, and will) to bless God, and as we do, there is the supernatural activation of soul prosperity. This is a practice that we must constantly do.

This is what God wants from us. There is no wonder as God spoke of David as a man of his own heart (1 Sam. 13:14; Acts 13:22). This was a special relationship with God, just as you also have as a prophet.

The mere fact that we may not have been entirely sold out on divine health as we submit to God may be news to some of us. Do we realize that God chooses us to do just this?

Where is our mind at in the process? Where is our will in this situation? Where are our emotions? Do we realize our status as God's chosen prophets? This is a great responsibility. Our souls must be ready and available for the task of God that lay ahead.

David is chosen of God, just as God chose us, and we now must walk in the fulfillment of that promise. David teaches us that we now learn how to see ourselves through the eyes of God. Again tell your soul to bless the Lord; you are in command of your soul. Speak to it.

Prophet, can you see your blood pressure as normal. Can you see yourself with no diabetes, no cancer? Can you see yourself with your weight under control? Let's keep speaking to our souls consistently.

Consistently is the key, and it will be a chore for most of us. I have taken hold of this, and I am in the process of exercising consistently as I encourage my soul now, just like David does. We need the promised benefits. We activate our souls for God's work.

Prophet, can you see yourself in divine health? Maybe you can see yourself free from any virus that manifests from anywhere. What disease is running through your lineage that you need to address? Prophet, this is serious business, and we need to get busy, like yesterday.

Prophet, this is faith at another level. We are leaving behind generational curses of what has run in our families. We are now embarking on a level of glory few of us have seen, imagined, or experienced.

Prophet, do you practice Romans 12:2?

"And be not conformed to this world: but be ye transformed by the renewing of your mind, that ye may prove what is that good, and acceptable, and perfect, will of God."

This is a necessary process. Renewing your mind is clearly what we are talking about here. This is a process to strengthen and mature our souls. We can't allow satan to continue to take from our souls over and over; we are being robbed.

God now lets us know what our soul has been robbed of. Satan wants us to be condemned with no way of escaping. Let's again pray for our health. We must know, claim, and keep speaking it. We must now claim that God makes our bodies. His intention for us is to be healthy when He created us.

We were designed to be healthy in the image of God. We have the dominion He has given us, and we are equipped to function healthily. Let me state something I stated in the previous chapter. We have to start from where we are at. We start here, and we move forward.

Consider this unbeatable combination: the power of the Word of God being spoken upon your life with the power and authority of someone determined to do the will of God. God knows when you mean business.

Are you ready to take this as a personal task upon yourself for your health? Tell your soul to bless the Lord over your sicknesses and diseases. Keep telling your soul to bless the Lord. We must practice changing the mind, which is critical for so many of us as it forces us to look at our health in another way.

The life-changing Word of God being spoken upon your life stirs and activates your soul to submit to the will of God. The byproduct of your health being in total harmony is with the will of God is priceless.

Prophet, do you want divine health? Do you want to turn it around and have a deposited experience? When we say we have to do the work, that is not a term to blow off or take lightly.

Do the work, prophet. Your spirit man and body led by your soul ushers in divine harmony. The product opium health upon your life is achieved. Prophets, there simply has never been a time like this; we find ourselves in a struggle to maintain our health daily.

Prophet, do you want it? Understand the key. We now know the enemy has attacked us through our souls and now we are taking action. The truth is that we can no longer be conformed to the world, but we must be transformed as we renew our minds. Let us never again allow our imagination to rule over us.

We can scream, holler, and speak about our faith, but we must do the work in our lives to be effective in God and where He wants us. Can we realize that we need to use our entire being to bless God?

Health is a divine benefit to us now, and we need it. Health is a vital part of our salvation. Let's be clear the anointing breaks the yoke of bad health. Good health results from a healthy soul at work, free from the fear of being sick, worry, failure, freedom to follow God, and see His salvation. We have just discovered how to activate good health with our souls as prophets of God.

Psalm 35 gives us additional perspective on faith and our soul. David knew that God was able. He could plead his case to God concerning his enemies.

Let's consider for a moment anything that hinders our health would be an enemy to our living. As you read Psalms 35, you see the pleading of David as he speaks to God to take over his soul.

Prophets are you willing to renew your life and health through your soul daily? This process can be boring until you develop a deeper relationship with God. This is a reality, and we must seek to do this. David has proved to be a great teacher in this aspect.

David pleads with God to stop the way against them that persecute me: say unto my soul, I am thy salvation. David has tapped into the knowledge of his soul. He knows that his soul is the key part of his life that needs to be convinced. This is real work and God's presence is the place to do just this.

David's soul, our souls, and the enemy of our health is seeking our soul. How many of us stand with David? He speaks for the activation of our souls to be active and aligned so that the enemy of our health will not be effective anymore. What am I talking about? Any type of urges, craves of whatever would raise itself to ruin our health.

While we see David speak about the enemy and how it has affected him, consider what and who has affected your health. Like David, prophet, our health has been an enemy, many times silent on the attack through the only portal available to it, and that is our souls.

The enemy identified in John 10:10 is clear to all of us. He is a thief stealing through our souls. Prophet, we must do the work to stop it. We can't afford to allow our souls not to be healthy.

Renew and we must deal with the soul blockers of gossip, rumor carriers, and backstabbers who believe they have a place in our lives. I am sure that you can name even more than I have listed.

The soul blockers come directly through your soul, and prophet, they block us while seeking to destroy. The goal is to destroy the total prophet, and health is a battlefield objective. Do you understand that our health is being destroyed?

My concern is that many of the prophets of God are subject to this. I have seen gifted prophets struggle with health concerns.

They can only stand so long, or they must get a certain amount of recovery time between sessions. Some prophets will only minister for a certain time due to health concerns.

This is troublesome because we are called to be difference makers. Should we not make a difference in our own lives? Let us realize we are not perfect, and we all need rest and to eat right. My concern is that our ministries are compromised by our health. We have to deal with this.

Many of us never tap into this revelation until we arrive late in our lives, if not at all. This has to stop. You are equipped, and I charge you to share and empower your fellow prophets.

You will do this with your actions, how you carry yourself, and the example you set. The understatement here is that you are being observed, and we must display the very character of God. We are leaders, which means we have to be examples. Leaders also need to relate to those we serve on this very topic. This is an important topic as the soul is clearly important in our health.

Psalms 42:6-7 is the very eloquence of God's Word, as David writes, my God, my soul is cast down within me. David says: therefore, will I remember thee from the land of Jordan, and the Harmonies, from the hill Mizar. The way David describes the deep speaks volumes. We now must understand that the soul gives us self-consciousness. This is the very essence of dealing with our health. We must be self-conscious about our health.

The soul is the only way. We now know that our souls alert us as prophets to be self-conscious of ourselves. Will you be responsible for yourself? Adam became self-aware of himself when God breathed into him. Self-consciousness gives us an awakening, feelings, and responsibility to take care of or maintain.

Grab the concept of understanding how important this is for a prophet. The soul is critical to operating as a prophet. It details the male or female mentality. The soul is the self-expression of the prophet. It has aspirations, feelings, and emotions.

The battle for your soul is your battle, prophet, even in these trying times of life. When you realize what the devil wants, you will understand the warfare. Again, the struggle is for your soul. This is what is controlling your health.

Have you realized that the devil's warfare in your life through your soul affects your marriage, ministry, relationships, world situations, and spiritual warfare?

We love to credit the devil for doing everything against us as prophets. We really need to avoid that and understand the actual tenants of warfare. The soul of a prophet is the battleground. The soul is the battleground, which means that we have some responsibility also.

The war in your mind that is going on in your soul is the war for your soul. We serve God with our mind, which is within the soul. You must get and understand this concept. When the mind is troubled, the soul is troubled.

When the prophet does not function properly in their mind, their soul is moved or unstable. None of the now day contemporary prophets can afford this. Our health is at stake.

This is the time prophets. We now speak to the forces that have hindered or wrecked our health. David called for these forces to be on a dark and slippery path, as the angel of the Lord persecuted them. David speaks that his joy would return through his soul.

The mentality of David teaches us that whatever keeps us from total soul prosperity is an enemy of God. Soul prosperity is enormous; it is the whole part of us. This is our health, wealth, true path to obtaining wisdom, and walking with our divine health.

Take all this into consideration. There will still be those who expect us to die. They will watch, and by their worldly observations, we are doomed. There is and probably will always be that mystique about the prophet. Prophet, trying to prove something to them is fruitless.

Apostle Paul shows us the mentality of a healthy soul. A healthy soul will operate even when there is a physical issue with the body. Keep reading, and understand this revelation of the soul and why they expect us to die.

CHAPTER 4

Prophet, Then Expect You To Die

We now know we are in a generation where we see a multitude of viruses. For various reasons, people are watching others suffer and possibly die. While the reasons are what they are, we are still blessed with the opportunity to live and serve God in good health.

Do we remember when a snake bit Paul? Acts 28:3 gives us a beautiful insight. The snake bites Paul as he shakes it off. The people stood there and speculated about Paul because he was expected to die.

As prophets, we deal with all different kinds of demonic entities. The snake was a test for Paul. The witch or the warlock who shows up at your meeting is a test for you, the prophet.

They come to watch you suffer, fail or even speculate on your demise. They strive to get into your mind and thoughts to rob you of your gift. They want to destroy you, and the gateway is your soul.

Do you remember the villagers in Acts 28 when Paul was in Malta? They talked about Paul, and they will do the same with you. Your ability to be prepared is vital. Paul shares this part of his life as a lesson that our health must be at a high level. There is always a reality of attack, whether you realize it.

Scripture says that the snake was poisonous, and the reality is that Paul should have been dead, but he did not die. His system was not affected. This has to be noticed by us all. He could walk into such a situation and handle himself. The prophet of today has the same type of warfare. We may very well not realize it until years have passed.

Today we see the health need. Health is needed to travel and convey the Word of God, the works of God, and the domain of God upon and to His people. This means that our souls must be like Paul. Was the soul of Paul in a place we should strive to be? The answer is yes!

We have far too many sick and unhealthy prophets ministering to people who come to us for healing. This is a true reality of the prophetic today. What do you think we are passing on to them? Do not get this confused with God using us because He will. Let's examine this issue even more.

Surely you have seen people who were leery of certain people laying hands on them. While there are several explanations, let us count the fact of being sick among the reasons listed. We, the prophets of God, are not the only ones with discernment. God does have people who can see and discern who are not necessarily prophets.

Prophets, we must get our souls well, so our health is in a divine status. Looking at Paul's life, seeing our lives, and knowing that our souls are prospering even as folks are looking at us and planning our demise, is that blessed assurance that God is with us. The snake bites Paul, and they wait for Paul to die, but the snake dies.

Paul demonstrates that our God heals and showers us with the benefits listed in Psalms 103:3-5. This is why David said to Bless the Lord; he commanded his soul to bless the Lord. We, as the new generation prophets, need to call out our souls and bless the Lord.

We are converting and controlling our souls and calling in the blessings of God. Prophets, because our health is spiritual, mental, and physical, we can't have one without the other. Prophet, this is past the time for us to stop our unfruitful habits.

We must now start to admit and understand that our health is what we think, eat, and believe. Our body has health laws, and we can't violate them anymore. Your soul is the leader of your health. Remember that you prosper and be in good health as your soul prospers. Prophets now's the time to get healthy.

There are clear benefits to our good health. We must also make sure that our soul is in love with God. Therefore, the soul is essential because it is the computer that connects us to the Holy Spirit and locks us into good health.

Let me be clear every prophet of this generation needs to lock into good health. This is simply priceless; there is no other way to describe it. We inherit the responsibility of good health within ourselves as the examples of His promise and the Glory. From Moses and every other prophet, know that this is a responsibility to live out.

This is a daily process as the prophet now submits his life to God. The soul is connected, and whatever God sends us, we are ready despite what the situation looks like. This is a vital part of the total preparation that the prophet needs.

Matthew 22:36 tells us to love God with our soul, and thus we release the Apostolic and Prophetic mantles of health upon our lives. Our obedience and submission will release health upon our lives. We should be assured to stay in the plan of God for our lives.

God is our maker and He controls our lives. God's revelation, revealing the promise of good health, will overrule anything that man says, contrary to our having good health. This means that we will allow God to lead us to a healthy place step by step. The Word of God will cover us with His grace, and health is a vital part of that.

I'm learning this daily and I encourage you to learn who you are health-wise and activate your soul. This is a vital area of your life.

Prophets, it is time for us to realize that our health has disgraced the entire body of Christ. This is the season now that we must take our health seriously in all manifestations of diseases and ailments. God wonderfully makes us.

Prophets, you were brought with a price; this is the time to get rid of lost hope. The need for good health is vital in each of our lives, and our souls are the key.

Consider the Spirit of God and what it does as you read this. You, prophet, seer, watchman, and Apostle, have been afforded a new opportunity for healing and deliverance. The enemy is looking for us to die. He has made plans because he knows we have not detected him stealing our health through our souls. Shout, "Glory," prophet, because now we have!

John 6:63 speaks to us that what God says about His Word is life. The words are life-producing. We ask God to search us in all areas including our souls (Psalms 139:23-24). Then God leads us to our healthy place.

Every prophet again needs to be healthy. This has to be our objective. We cannot keep ministering to people, and we are not even close to being healthy, and we don't know why? Our souls are missing the needed mentality of divine health status. Why would the now generation trust us? We are what they see, can you imagine that?

The mentality of good health has to be practiced. This is what happens naturally when we train ourselves to love God. Our souls must love God. When taken over by our lusts, imagination, and negative thoughts, our souls will keep us sick.

Recently we lost one of our prophets. She was known for her mentality, even through her personal illness. She was a known prayer warrior. Throughout our working together, she grew in soul prosperity and helped many people.

She also saw the need for her to change so she could grow. There is no doubt in my mind that she lived longer because of her soul growth. She went from a shy prophetic gift to a national prophetic intercessor who God used mightily.

We show God as we present our souls to Him that we are willing to change. This is the necessary personal changes we discussed in previous chapters. Prophets, are we willing to change our minds to get healthy?

We must remember that the soul is the opening. We are not sick through the spirit or the body, but the opening, computer, processor, and soul is the opening for the enemy to keep us sick. What is our soul dealing with, and are we using the tool of God to reclaim our health?

The body follows the soul; it is designed that way. Matthew 22:37-40 demonstrates that the soul is the foundation of all spiritual laws and prophetic utterances.

Prophets, we must love God with all our hearts and souls; this is the first and the great commandment. We can't overlook the fact. This is the key to our health.

This is why the body will follow the soul, and if the soul does not demonstrate love for God, then the body will reflect what looks like death in the natural. Remember David says, "Bless the Lord, Oh, my soul." Once again, we see the soul being activated. Challenge your soul prophet, and it will change. Say it now, "devil, your days of stealing my health are over." Shout it and mean it!

Indeed, we all have seen people who are gifted and ready to prophesy, and after or sometimes before, they reflect death. They are so tired and taking different medications.

The gift is there, but the love of God is lacking, and it reflects upon the vessel of God. We have to love God enough to want to take care of ourselves and maintain divinely healthy bodies.

Prophets, the pathway to your destiny, is your soul; everybody will not understand it, nor will they all accept it. This has not been a mainstream prophetic issue, but as you read this book, I challenge you to make it one. Make it one for yourself first. Prophet, become the first partaker, and then you can be the example.

Today's prophets have their own selfish motives, and this is something we can't be selfish with. This is our health. We have to learn how to give of ourselves. This is a soul issue that we have to solve and teach others. Every one of us, as the now day prophets, has work to do in this area.

While we strongly seem to want everyone in agreement with our moves, don't be discouraged if they are not. Your health is a cause before you that is far too important and big.

The now generation thinking points to us to become heroes, if only in our own mind. Prophet, our health is a soul issue that hurts us and has to change. Can you see why we are so often under attack? Do we realize this hurts our health?

Let us look through the Body of Christ, and you will see the differences in prophets who will become sacrificial prophets and give of themselves versus the prophets who will not become martyrs for God because they feel the cause does not elevate them enough. This is the line of thinking of a soul under attack and does not realize it.

There's a relevant lack of understanding of soul prosperity, and we wonder why our health is in the target zone. Let us work within the prophetic community to make it commonplace to connect and discern our greatest threat: our souls being invaded.

Remember David standing and facing his older brother and telling him that there is a reason to be concerned. There are legitimate reasons to be concerned about our health, prophets.

We have a responsibility to understand what our soul is doing related to our personal health. They may expect us to die or drop dead, but our ability to be prepared will have us stand as Paul did.

We must build on the power of relationships. Some opportunities we will never know about because we are not ready. Could our health be the reason we are not ready?

There is a shortage of prophets today walking in divine health. We need to cheer and help each other. We are conditioned that it's not about me, then it is not God. That is a selfish attitude, and we do not want to open up to what God has sent to us because we feel it is not about us. The revelation of our being empowered is needed.

Prophets let us understand that there is a shortage of sacrifice today in the Body of Christ. The shortage starts and ends with us. David shows us what it means to be vested in Christ.

Like all of us, David had his faults but the fact that he was not totally focused on his own pleasure or motives is a great trait to show him as an example to prophets everywhere. Again the question, "Is there not a cause?" David says, "you persecute me but is there not a cause?"

CHAPTER 5

The Prophet's Soul Persecution

Dealing with the world is one thing, and dealing with yourself is another. How about when there is persecution concerning your soul towards the world. One of our most outstanding issues in the prophetic is understanding how to protect our souls. Safeguarding your mind, will, and emotions is a real issue.

When we fail to protect our soul, our spirit becomes invalid. This is a natural progression. Psalms 143:3-4 describes the issue before us now. The persecution of the soul and what seems to be the death of the spirit with us. Have you ever experienced this dryness within yourself?

Prophet, think for a minute and consider what I have been continuously speaking. Satan attacks your soul before he will attack your body. The soul is the opening. This is where he must come through. I have discussed this point numerous times in this book. This must become real to you.

Satan can only persecute your soul, not your spirit. This puts your soul in a spiritual prison (Psalms 142:7). You must bring your soul out. The soul is the key again; we see the enemy with his crafty ways attack but always through the soul.

Prophet, now understands that we are sick because our percussed souls could not feed or be nourished, and we find ourselves suffering. David cried unto the Lord and said, "Bring my soul out of prison so I can give God the glory."

Prophet, can you understand that once your soul is freely submitted, God has spoken that He will bountifully bless you. This equates to a pure soul that we see illustrated in Matthew 5:8.

Blessed are the pure in heart. The soul and the heart are one and the same. The heart is the actual storage space of the soul, the place where our deepest secrets and feelings live.

Every prophet needs the goal that now is the time to make divine health steps even amid our haters and especially our persecutors. The prophet must become a student of their personal divine health steps.

These steps start with our soul.

God wants to trust His prophet to make divine health steps that are necessary to get us ready for servitude. Each prophet must now ask themselves, "Is this a divine health step for me? Have I clearly articulated my motives through my soul?" This is about relationship prophet; there is no substitute for it. The challenge awaits, does the prophet want divine health or not.

This will be a process to change our thinking and change how we communicate with God. Our focus must be profound for a deeper divine health status that we seek. We have to change, which means that it will require some work on our part.

The work starts as we speak to God. Create in me a clean heart which is the cleansing of the soul. We have quoted that scripture for years, and many of us need to be aware of the soul and heart relationship.

Psalm 51:10 illustrates: create in me a clean heart and renew the right spirit. Notice the order, the heart (soul), and the spirit is renewed. This will not happen unless the soul is in proper order. The soul must be trained; a computer must be programmed in the same aspect.

Prophet, do you understand that this is our task for ourselves. In Romans 12:2, the renewing of the mind is critical. This tells us that we now have a responsibility to ensure our souls are in the proper standing.

How many of you can see that this is possible for you? Say now to yourself, "Bless the Lord oh, my soul and all that is in me." Encourage your soul to bless the Lord.

We can see that we, as prophets, must be ready in all areas of our life, especially our health. How often have we ignored the process of cleansing or commanding our souls to activate good health? Maybe a better question is, did we even know this?

We want good health, but what is the process we will endure for divine health? The forces of satan have launched out against us through our souls. We live to a point, and then changes come into our lives.

Education is crucial, and we must adhere to it and practice the process. How many of us have been taught about divine health? The reality is that most of us have not been taught about divine health, especially in relationship to prophetic assignments.

A reality that not all will admit but presents a fight to overcome. We must teach and practice the right we have to divine health. Our work for God depends on it.

Let me be very clear on this. We will still have challenges in our bodies, and yet unless we know our divine rights and our soul issues, we are doomed to live in trouble.

I want to ask the question again. Do you believe that divine health is possible for you? Prophet, do you believe divine health is necessary for you to be effective in ministry? You will not work on what you do not believe in. That is a fact.

Look at your body and whatever shape you're in; know that your body did not do it. Your soul did. You must know that your soul will listen to God or the devil. This is upon us prophets to work with our souls. Let us work hard to learn this.

Is your body out of control? It was only following suit. Your body depends on your soul, and if your soul is not in full complete operation, this is what you can expect. Your soul is on the witness stand, and it is without faith. God did not call everyone to the position you are in prophet. He did however call you!

What is clear is Matthew 9:17. How many of us think that we looked at it in the physical sense? Can we not see that ignoring the old for too long will always lead to decay?

I am saying that we have ignored our bodies for far too long, and we want to be helpers and heroes to others, so, we must be the first partakers of what we are willing to share and help others with.

How many of us realize that the soul's health is the key to the body's health. In the introduction of this book, you needed to understand this is a process.

There is no doubt that some will read this and maybe become discouraged because the process will not produce a microwave result. Please do not be a fool my friend. Only an unrealistic person would expect that, yet I know some will.

Godly results will consistently reproduce after Godly work. We know this as the scripture tells us that each will produce after its kind. Do not expect a peach tree to produce bananas; it will not happen.

When we give God a half effort, we get undesired results. We want God's best, and we must earn it. Our health is on the line, and it is beyond priceless; it is vital.

Let us deal with some food for thought. While we see things in people's lives, have you ever thought your perspective of what you see is what God wants to do in your life? Let us apply what we know now about the soul to this.

Many of the prophets today are looking at what they see, and we find fault and error in each other. The reality is that God has us in the problem for the problem to work on us.

Paul prays that the eyes of our understanding would be enlightened. We are too busy responding to our flesh and not operating in the light. We have a shortage of light. This is why the prophet today is blinded, especially in understanding the soul.

How we perceive a situation is critical. We must understand it has to get light, or we will live in the valley of dark regret.

The situation here is living in regret about our health. My prayer is that not another prophet lives in regret and struggle with health issues and be in service to God at the same time.

Yes, I realize we will be challenged, but we are given the option to control our soul activity, which is priceless. This is the value of a restored soul.

In Ephesians 1:15-23, Apostle Paul is praying that God would give us a needed spirit of wisdom and revelation. This is the key to the true knowledge of Him. In Ephesians 1:18-19, Paul elaborates on what that means. God wants us to know the essentials about our salvation that will assure us about our high calling as His people.

This includes the prophets of God. The hope and eternal perspective to endure trials are the tools of God He uses to give us the strength to persevere in godliness.

Did it ever occur that God wanted you to change your perspective of that person? In other words, when you changed your perspective, you benefitted from the learning experience. Instead of seeing just the fault, you also saw the reason why. You have effectively seen yourself in your own personal pit.

CHAPTER 6

Prophet, Escaping The Pit Your Soul Created

Your very life as a prophet is filled with transition. We always have a starting point: when it started and where we move from. One of the absolute hardest issues in the life of a prophet is how to move through the transitions of life and be effective without falling flat on your face.

I have been talking about the soul and its effect on our health. Do we realize by now that soul health is also critical to our physical health and our spiritual health?

Dealing with the things in life daily puts us in a place where we seem to attract the most drama and attention unlike the other fivefold gifts. That leads to more than our share of confusion, misunderstanding, and a buffet of feelings from not being called to having our head so swollen that no one seems to recognize the new and improved you.

Many of the things that happen in our life as prophets are actually so we can be a blessing to someone else. The issue is hard because we may see ourselves as anointed, but the transition of where we are at is a mental process for every prophet. The soul, at this point, has not adequately learned to process the information we need to grow and maintain our health.

Mentally if you're not open to growth, there is a reality that you will ignore and always blame others for what is not in your life. What's sad is that you will never take any responsibility for it. This is why so many prophets make and have excuses. They do not experience soul prosperity, which means their health will eventually suffer also, as they do spiritually.

Prophets, as the soul develops, remember this fact. The reality of your instincts will always see you further along than you are, but you will never take responsibility because your uncomfortable reality is your pit. People who know you will look at you and see the gift; they will sometimes want to tap into your gift. You will get excited, but there will be no growth.

While I am detailing a long-term effect, I find this is an issue that so many prophets have been through, and as they age, they see no need to develop their souls to ensure good health.

With no personal growth, your gift will become stagnate over time because it transitions into a burden, and you spend your time worrying and being irritated because your instincts are telling you there is more, but you can't find it. We are responsible, and yet how many of us really know that we are?

This now becomes your norm. The enemy of God benefits from your normal of no growth, is a mental pit and absolute anger, frustration, and irritation that you exhibit and never can fulfill your destiny because mentally, you're in a pit.

There is a sadder reality here and that is in the prophetic community, we have not taught enough about the personal pit of a prophet. The concept is strange and foreign to us, just like the development of our soul.

We must do a better job of letting every prophet, seer, apostle, watchman, and gift of the prophetic community know we can get out of the pit that our soul creates.

Can we consider that we have been so entangled with the familiar in our life that we have labeled it the natural, and many times more often than not, it is not the natural? Consider that our instincts tell us there is more, God has more for us, but our intelligence tells us that we need to learn more about God. Our relationship with God must be strengthened above and beyond what we consider to be comfortable.

We want to be in a comfortable place with God, and He is calling us to a place in the deep. Do we trust God with all our souls to keep us in the right place in our life, including being healthy? This is a serious issue to be concerned about, especially as a prophet.

Those of you in the process of transitions right now in your life will find the reality that your experience will contradict your instincts. Your experience will warn you, but your instincts will have you still move in other directions. Let's look at our health as one of those other directions.

Moving to a place guided by your instincts but not validated by your experiences is ongoing. Something is wrong; you're built for more, but your experiences limited you, and that is a reality you can't ignore.

Our soul and health has been blocked. This is destroying the prophetic community that many have never imagined. The reality is that our soul has been attacked, and we do not seem to be aware of it.

Every one of us has a personal type of pit. We are captive to sin and the issues in our lives. In Psalms 51:5, David speaks of his personal situation because he realizes his pit. He says, "I was brought forth in iniquity/sin, and in sin did my own mother conceive me." David knew he was an outside child and he needed to maintain good soul health to do what God called him to do.

David realized that his mother had a relationship with someone who was not Jessie. We see how he speaks of his personal sin in verses 1-4, but in verse 5, he now identifies his mother and her actions in relation to her situation.

His pit is the reality of living as a stepson and being different, treated differently from his brothers. Psalms 69:5-12 tells us of his deep inner feelings, his instincts about how he sees his situation, and his discomfort for being there and knowing that it is his reality.

His instincts are rebuked by what has happened and what is happening to him. David teaches us that his soul is awakened to the reality of his life at this time.

What do you do, prophet, when all of your experiences validate the place you are in your life, but you have instincts that keep telling you to go higher? They keep nagging, speaking to you that there is more for you.

Can you relate? Can you see the reality of the place you're at? Can you discern that there is more for you? Can you see that your instinct is telling you that you're not crazy? You are just in transition. Prophet, do you trust your soul where you are at today? Are you a prophet in the process of going from point A to point B?

There is a roar within you for greater, and it does not matter where you're from, how big, tall, or short you are. There is no barrier to your race, culture, or nationality. You have to summon it up within you.

You can't stay within the pit forever; it is like a prison to you. You know you need to get out, but the question is, are you ready to come out of your pit by any means that God deems necessary? This, for the prophet, is what faith is about, being called to an unknown place and being able to trust God. Soul development is at a premium at this point.

Prophet, is your soul in a self-created pit for you? Are you walking in the blessings of prosperity to include good health? Do you see yourself humble enough to know you did nothing to merit it? Yet it is different, unknown, and if it happened earlier in your life, you would have probably spoken out that it was not of God. It was the devil. Why? Because we don't seem to understand the importance of the soul in our lives. We will blame everyone and everything for what we do not understand.

The prophet in the pit that your soul created is a learned behavior. Making due, getting by is a learned process, but if you can learn that, you can learn how to handle more, and even more than enough.

You can learn how to handle it because you are called out of the pit. We are discussing health in this book because we can learn how to improve our health and do it now.

The reality of prophets going through their lives supporting a system of not enough, supporting the theology of just enough, or having anymore is simply not of God and contradicts His Word. God has given us the option to obtain good health, and we need to establish soul prosperity for it.

Jesus said that I have come for you. He wants us to experience and have life and have it more abundantly. Are you supporting a system in your life that the Word of God disputes? Why are you supporting this system, and do you realize your soul is a portal that needs to be adjusted?

Is the pit created by your soul so comfortable that you have lost your ambition to come out, or do you have none? You must answer these questions, then you can answer are you prepared to come out of your pit or stay in the system of mental anguish and bathe daily in the water of inability? This will be a sign you are ready to operate in divine health because you will not allow your health to lag anymore.

How many of us realize that we have spent too much time, invested too much energy and resources in pits that we never intended to capture or live in? The enemy has been busy in our lives. We, the prophets, have missed the promises of God in our attempts to help others.

You are called to nations, regions, countries, cultures, and even faiths. Your gift transcends the norm and God is saying the time is now! This means everything must be a go-to, including our health.

Learning is a constant process; it is a process that will support you on every level in life you go to. Those of you who refuse to stretch will never understand that the ceiling of one level is the floor of the next level. You will understand that our whole life is about training and preparing for the next. Our health seems to never become an issue until we are shown the need. This usually comes from our bad health or someone we know as having problems health-wise.

Prophets this is about learning how to operate in a new and different environment. We have to use those acquired skills of the pit and what it represented in our lives to come out, be effective in our moving forth, and become an exponent of change in the lives of the one to who we have been assigned. Has your soul shown you that you can be an exponent of change?

Prophet, are you ready to go to another level? It will be different; it will look unlike anything you have seen before. Even the quality and methods of communication will be different. You will not be able to relate on the level you related to in your past. Prophet, your soul will allow you to see, hear and feel the difference. Get ready for a difference.

The most awesome thing you can experience out of your pit is a new opportunity. It is powerful, and it is a reality that you must seize and trust God with to keep moving forth. This is so powerful as now you have the opportunity to recreate yourself in the aspect of becoming a better prophet, seer, apostle, or watchman. This means that you can see the total aspect of yourself, especially your health.

Here is where you understand that people who knew you in the pit are now exposed to you outside the pit, and they recognize your growth. They now generate that needed respect you sought, but you never knew how to get it from them because now you're out of your pit. This is a fact that you are growing, and you can take responsibility.

There is still a reality that we can mess up the new assignment with our old habits. Our old habits will allow the same curse to follow us, so we have to be sharp and in the presence of God constantly.

The reality of climbing out of our individual pits is a daunting task, and we have to appreciate the process of trusting God on our blind faith. This is why as prophets, we must be willing to leave things in our lives and move forth. Understanding that in season A, there were things I learned and did that may not be necessary for season B.

Once the prophet has grown out of the pit his soul has created, they are introduced to learn a whole new set of perspectives and principles for the new level they have ascended to.

I am out of the pit, and if I don't be careful, I will fall into another pit at another level. This is why learning never stops. Blaming the devil for everything that has happened in your life is not what God wants us to realize or process. We must take responsibility as much has been invested in you, and much is expected of you. This is why this chapter has been presented to you. My goal was to get you to understand the actions outside of the health that has kept us from developing divine health.

There is yet another concept we need to know as we move from our personal pit of nothing. Prophet, you are called to be an element of change and to understand that it must happen in your life. Whatever is in your life that refuses to change, drop it! Let me say that again, drop it!

You can't be held back or held by what refuses to change. We are to be transformed as our mind renews (Romans 12). You're ready, and you need to change. Prophet, you are changing, becoming a prophet of relevance that God will use, but not if you do not change. When you change, your soul is the proof of the change. We must change our mindset so our souls will inherit the prosperity God has for us.

Finally, as we look at the pit of our souls, there is not a comfortable way for you to move forth as God has called you to a place that even you do not understand, and many are speaking against it. This is important because if you really want to lose the pit mentality and the theology of the pit, then you need to lose what it represents in your life.

Those of you who have to look around to see if others agree before deciding will find yourself like blind Bartimaeus as he sat by the road waiting for Jesus to show up. He was willing to shed his coat and achieve his sight. What are you willing to shed to achieve your destiny, prophet? Now that you have understood this, are you ready to generate soul prosperity? You must reread this chapter if you do not. The issue is that serious. Do that before you read about how a deposited experience will feed your soul. Bottom line: let's get healthy.

CHAPTER 7

Prophets Living With Deposited Experiences And How They Feed Your Soul

2 Corinthians 5:5 says, "God has made us for His purposes and His Spirit as a deposit. The Spirit is guaranteeing what is to come." Prophet, not many things in life are truly guaranteed.

What we have here today can be gone tomorrow, Prophet. Let's now discuss our health based on the many factors that our soul deals with. We'll now discuss areas we need to get in order for our souls to prosper. This is very important as we will need to have our souls in shape to secure the level of health we need.

Buy something and get a "guarantee" it comes with conditions. In Romans 8:29, there is a divine purpose that the Apostle Paul goes to great lengths to let us know that God has done something huge to guarantee our future. The phrase "what is to come" stands for all of God's promises, including our health.

God is so particular about it and committed to His own purposes. God made a "deposit" in us that guarantees "what is to come." Every battle we have with sin purifies our soul so that heaven will not seem foreign to us.

I have discussed why the soul is the opening to sin in our lives, and it is the key to everything that happens in our lives. So when we put our health on the line, we must know that our health is part of the guarantee. This is why a deposited experience to us is critical. This is about feeding the soul so we can prosper in all areas of our lives, especially our health.

God's Deposited Experiences is serious business. The Holy Spirit is God's "personal deposit" in our lives. Then, guarantee He will one day finish what He has started in our lives. The gift of His Spirit is that God has made a down payment on our future salvation. Prophet, imagine that the "deposit" lies in your future intentions. So now I ask you what your intentions are about your health. Prophet, realize that your soul will ultimately answer that question about you.

Consider the Holy Spirit as God's "investment" in you. The divine purpose of God is clearly working in each of our lives now. The "good work" (Philippians 1:6) in us the moment we trusted Christ. Prophet, our divine purpose as His servants involves being shaped into the image of Jesus (Romans 8:29). We must be healthy.

The Spirit of God is working in us if our souls are submitted to it. Think about our great blessings. Blessings that already are ours because we have the Spirit. The Spirit that is indwelling is doing several things. Things like making intercession, giving comfort, guidance, and security. These are full rights as God's servants.

Yet, we see these things, as good as they are, are only the down payment or "first fruits." When you consider this, you now can just imagine what God will yet do for His prophets.

Prophet, adopt this quick prayer. "Oh Lord, you know already about everything that will happen to me today. Please allow me to be thankful for everything that happens in my life today, in Jesus' name. Amen."

Proverbs 29:18 speaks of a key concept for prophets today. Where there is no vision, people will perish. A prophet that can see is common in the world, but a prophet with vision is rare. Vision is a unique ability to see beyond where our eyes can look. You need the vision to see yourself healthy. That means you have a healthy foundation in your life called the soul.

We all know people who spend their ministry time complaining about their personal health. They do not have a vision for this but will want to pray and proclaim blessings for others. God uses prophets and seers who are open to His will and way. Their souls are open and available for His use.

God is the giver of wisdom and knowledge. Wisdom and knowledge will change our lives. You can be sure that you have everything you need to move to your next level, and that is through deposited experiences He takes us through as prophets.

As prophets, we are constantly growing and changing. We should mature and become more like Christ. The maturing process affects all areas of life, including new spiritual assignments. Do you feel God is preparing you for greater things? This does not happen unless the soul can process the changes of the deposited experience. Everything moves through the soul.

Let's look at Samuel 17:31-37; David has been brought before Saul. News of David's bold words about how Goliath had to be faced has him before the king. David expresses that he can and will fight Goliath. King Saul sees it as an impossible task because of his youth and vast inexperience.

David shares his story of fighting against a lion and a bear. He explains how they had attempted to rob sheep from the flock he was entrusted to watch. This was David's deposited experience.

We also see a critical lesson that David learned in the process. David says that a lion came and took a sheep from the flock. He went after the lion and smote (or struck) it.

Whatever he used, it was enough to apparently either knock the lion in a place where he could be seriously distracted. David then had enough time and opportunity to rescue the poor sheep out of the lion's mouth.

After the magnificent rescue, however, the lion arose and attacked David. David had hand-to-hand combat (or hand-to-paw) with the lion. He won the fight and killed the lion.

The deposited experience of David showed that he had learned a critical lesson from these experiences: finish your enemy while he is down. Call it merciless and brutal, but in war, one does not always have the chance to negotiate. David was physically fit, and his deposited experiences were needed to put himself in this position. His soul had processed the required information for him to be successful.

The enemy does not want you to have that opportunity to be successful. We see so many prophets stuck in the moment because they do not understand that the soul is important in this process.

When a Philistine plans to kill you and subject your nation to slavery and humiliation, you don't think twice about it. David didn't. He struck down Goliath to the ground, just like the lion.

But then he immediately went over, took the Philistine's sword, and severed his head. This time, there would be no chance for the enemy to leap up and counterattack.

This is why some prophets continue to take the same test repeatedly and never seem to understand why. You must pass the test. What is coming through our souls, and what are we willing to let go to move ahead? We must deal with the deposited experiences to be done with sin. Does this have anything to do with your health, prophet?

This has everything to do with your health, prophet. Who wants to be a slave to our lust for things that are prone to make us slaves to desires and passions which will devour and destroy our health? We must be done with weights that will hinder our walk with God. Prophet, wherever you are at this moment in your life, say: "God, I want to go to my new level, and I am willing to go through the tests."

Here are ten principles to help you understand the processing of a deposited experience as they feed your soul daily. Keep in mind that if the soul is not operating healthily, then other areas of your life will be ineffective. Again, let me stress that this whole chapter is about the soul as it is fed and processes information. Let's now look at ten essential points of a fed soul.

Getting your life in order will go a long way to getting your health in order. I have focused on health and the prophet's soul importance so far. Let's now look at these other areas that work along with a prophet's health. These areas need to be in line just as the health is also. The prophet will focus on his health and realize that they are professionals for God. The following ten areas are critical for a healthy soul foundation.

#1 Be Convinced God Is Calling You; If Your soul Is Disturbed, You Will Be Confused

When God begins the process of elevating His prophets, they go through a transition and must be thoroughly convinced that He is calling them. They need to be secure in His plans and purposes for their lives as best as they understand them.

There can and will struggle; there will be things you don't always understand or can make sense out of. Prophet, when you know deep down inside your heart that God has called you, nothing can convince you otherwise. You understand that this is God's destiny for you. Understand you will be tested.

There are times when only your conviction of your call will be what you can draw on when facing hardships. Every prophet will deal with this in some form. If you're going to deal with change effectively, listen to this. You must persevere through hardships. Being convinced is not debatable. This is the norm. You are walking according to your assigned call as a prophet or what you have received. Welcome to your prophetic call. Can we now assume that you are convinced? Are you convinced that no matter what happens, you will not quit on God and yourself?

This conviction is needed in your heart that God has called you to this transition and change. This will give you the determination to succeed regardless of personal costs. Our awesome God declares the end from the beginning. You should shout victory now (Is 46:10). God knew already what the outcome of our situation was going to be before He brought you into this world.

#2 Understand The Power Of A Prophetic Word In Your Life And What It Means For Your Soul.

Sometimes we see God place us in troublesome surroundings, but it is all part of His plan. In Acts 21:10-12, a prophet named Agabus came to Paul. He took Paul's belt and bound his own feet and hands with it. That had to be a sight. Agabus says, "The Holy Spirit declares, 'the owner of this belt be bound by the Jewish leaders, and then he will be turned over to the Gentiles.'" When they heard this, the local believers and others begged Paul not to go on to Jerusalem.

Paul is given a prophetic word, and those who heard this word assumed it was a word to warn Paul not to go. Paul knew he was meant to go. Acts 22:22-24 says, "And now I am bound by the Spirit to go to Jerusalem. I don't know what awaits me except that the Holy Spirit tells me that jail and suffering lie ahead in the city after city." Paul reflects on his life. He knows his life is worth nothing unless he will finish the work assigned to him by the Lord Jesus.

The prophetic word was not a word of warning, but a word of confirmation about what he was sensing would lie ahead. This experience shows that Paul knew what was ahead, and he allowed God to prepare him to deal with what lay ahead in his life. Paul was effectively able to process the prophetic word in his life. Paul had a deposited experience through his soul. The importance of this can't be overlooked.

#3 Understand That Your deposited Experience Has Laid A Foundation For Your Next Assignment, And Your Soul Will Process It For Your Readiness.

God builds upon what He has done within you, what you have been through, and how you went through it. Prophet, you are His temple, and upon you He builds. Look at your life, and you can see the patterns of what God is doing. View your experiences as places where God has prepared you there for greater. The deposit experience shows you are being equipped for your next place in God.

God will, on purpose, expand you in those specific areas or build upon the foundation already in you. Learn from not dwelling in your past failures and pain. God uses those experiences to prepare you for your future. Prophet, your messes become a message, and your trials become a testimony. Trust that God already knows the outcome; He gives us glimpses of the outcome in visions.

#4 Evaluate What You Need To Change, What You Take Into Your Soul, And What You Refuse To Process Through Your Soul.

We need to pray and read the Word much more than we do. These things are part of the process, but they are not the only part of the process. God leading will take you to the next level, and you will begin to discern specifics about your new assignment. This is a different kind of preparation but still a part of your deposited experience.

Eliminate any financial debt or break unholy alliances so you can survive as you build your ministry. These are simply examples of tying up loose ends in your life. You must be free to go to where He is leading you. Sometimes emotional attachments have to be broken so you can start your new assignment. Evaluate what must be changed in the natural world and allow God to start changing those things in your life. You do know this includes your health also.

#5 Understand There Will Be Opposition, And Your Soul Will Be Attacked.

Because God has called you to do something, does not mean it will be easy. No great man or woman of God is exempt from the opposition. We see Jesus was opposed by the devil, religious leaders, and even His friends and family. Prophet, you need to commit to overcoming opposition. Opposition is a vital deposits experience. Change will bring challenges.

Opposition will always come, somehow, some-way in subtle ways. Opposition will attempt to sidetrack us. Opposition has an assignment itself; you must first overcome it. Prophets, the Word tells us that God will show up and blow our minds (Hab. 1:5).

#6 Utilize A Mentor to Help Feed Your Soul and Move You To The Next Level

The Kingdom of God is built on earth by the greatness of God's servants who serve. They become that way through the influence of other great men and women of God in their lives. The sooner you see the value of mentorship, the quicker you will succeed in God.

We see that Barnabas mentored Paul. We also see that Paul mentored Timothy, Titus, and others. Wisdom and knowledge that a mentor can share and impart to you are invaluable.

Having a mentor is needed. They will walk with you and help you mature in your ministry. You will be allowed to fail and not doubt God's call. Welcome to the learning and growing phase of your life.

Proper alignment with a mentor is needed to fulfill your destiny and is vital to your getting to the next level. Mentors are an invaluable resource in a prophet's life. The deposited experience that they download is critical to your success.

#7 Understand You're A Threat To The Kingdom of Darkness Because Of The Warfare You Have Dealt With Through Your Soul.

God shows us His vision because He wants us to be visionaries by writing the vision down for others to see and to be blessed from it as well. As a prophet, the more you walk into God's plans and purposes, the more you will come under enemy's fire. Prophet, you are a genuine and credible threat to the kingdom of darkness, and you become a target because of that.

The deposited experience of being a target can be bothersome and make some prophets shy away from the call. This is normal, and it does not signify that you're doing something wrong. On the contrary, you are doing something right! Oh, that enemy will attack your soul to worry and frustrate you.

Prophets, even though we know that the enemy of our souls is a defeated foe, there is still a battle raging. You must know and expect to be attacked when we are making headway into areas that he is controlling. Attacks of our opposition will intensify when we move from one level to the next. Embrace a new season and take on your new assignment for God. Warfare will always follow because the enemy wants to stop us from doing what we are called to do to advance God's Kingdom.

#8 God Called You, Man Did Not, So Submit Your Soul

Prophets, entering into their new assignment from the Lord, are overwhelmed. The assignment seems so much bigger than what they feel capable of or feel they deserve even. This was not your choice. God enables those that He calls period. Accept that the decision was God's and not yours.

The anointing and authority that you haven't experienced will start to show up in your life. God did call you. Accept that decision and be humble. When you embrace that God called you and remain humble, you will be able to focus and deal with your distractors. This deposited experience will sharpen your focus. Here is the capital reason we are attacked in our souls because God called us. This is plain and really simple.

#9 Embrace the Process of Change; It Begins In Your Soul.

Do you realize that God has designed change to be a process, not an event? Too often, we parade change as an event, but it is a process of the "Deposited Experience' received through your soul as we move to our next level.

God is not in a hurry. He allows His prophets time to process the changes that He is making. God is certainly interested in the result of the changes that He orchestrates in our lives. The process of growth and maturity accompanies change that is also vital to God.

God works diligently, deliberately, and more slowly than most prophets want! God has perfect timing and a grand plan for your life. It will bring you great joy and fulfillment if you will patiently cooperate with it.

Our society expects instant results to go along with our instant potatoes. God just doesn't work in that manner. He is the master-builder of lives piece by piece. Prophet, if we rush the process, there will be weaknesses in our lives. We will have to deal with those weaknesses later because you didn't allow God to place all the pieces you need into your life.

#10 Be Bold, Be Strong, For The Lord Your God Is With You

Any time you are going to move forward with God, there comes a time when you finally have to go for it. You must learn that you have to take that step of faith. This is the step beyond commitment, decision making, and of no return. It is when you finally put action to your calling.

Whenever God shows us His plan (vision), and we write it down, we can take it to the bank. It is already done in eternity; it simply has yet to manifest itself in time. We must wait confidently that the visions will come to pass.

God is not a liar, trust that fact (Numbers 23:19), so if He tells you something will happen, it will! The Apostle James puts it this way. He said in James 2:26, For as the body without the spirit is dead, faith without works is also dead. You can study, commit, and decide until the cows come home, but it is all for naught if you do not step out in faith.

Stepping out into this level of faith requires a step into the supernatural. We will get healthy. Let's proclaim it.

I trust that your soul is healthy after reading this, or you are making a real decision to submit your soul based on this chapter. This is clearly a supernatural process and let's discuss it now.

CHAPTER 8

The Prophets Soul and The Atmosphere of The Supernatural

The atmosphere is a pervading tone or mood of a place. "Supernatural" is defined as being "beyond nature" and cannot be compelled by nature. "The supernatural" does cancel out and contradict "nature." The supernatural enhances the natural as in an atmosphere to a whole new level is realized. This atmosphere is one where the gifts of the Spirit flow with miracles, signs, and wonders. This is the atmosphere of the Supernatural.

God gives His prophets the grace to build the spiritual atmosphere so that we can charge it with faith, worship, and expectation. Worship, faith, and expectations will change the atmosphere into the supernatural. This means that your soul aligns with what God wants to do.

As prophets, we can change the atmosphere by speaking prophetic words of life, which create a unique physical environment. A distinctive atmosphere is the birthplace of supernatural miracles. The physical environment around you is the atmosphere of your life.

So understand that the word of the prophet has power and the authority to change the physical environment. Here is where we need to focus, as we are a part of the physical environment. We can change our health. We have the power and the authority to do just that.

This book will require you to study and reread to capture the essence of the function of the soul in the process of our health. We have focused on everything around us, and we have not allowed our souls to elevate our health.

This is the season we do just that. Speak to your issues, decree, and declare as a supernatural atmosphere manifests. Most people believe it when they see it. Prophets believe it before other people see it because they've already seen the outcome in the Spirit.

Let us start to see ourselves well and healthy in the Spirit. This means our soul must be fully committed to God for this to happen to see ourselves in the spirit realm.

As prophets, we discern and perceive things in the Spirit realm others do not. God has allowed us to specialize in revealing His "secret counsel" in His timing. Amos 3:7 surely justifies that God speaks to His prophets before He reveals His secrets to the world.

Our souls must be sensitive. Certain things in life will impact the atmosphere around a prophet. Things like region, history, culture, strongholds, and expectations or a lack of them all have a significant effect.

We all have factors from our past still affecting how we live and function. There also are things taking place right now that may be affecting the atmosphere around you right now. These things like family or your personal life all come into play. Yes, there are many more that we all could name.

Despite all these things, God can change an atmosphere through your ability to communicate. Prophets, you are an atmosphere changer! This is a craft we must work on, just like speaking to our health is a habit we must establish in each of our lives.

Words will change the atmosphere. They are waiting on us to use them. Remember the woman in 2 Kings 4:1-4 who cried out to Elisha. Her husband was dead, and the creditor wanted to take her sons to pay off the husband's debt.

Elisha asked her what she had. She only had a jar of oil. She and the boys did as Elisha instructed. They borrowed pots and pans. They poured oil from the small jar. Her situation changed because of one word. The word was obedience.

An atmosphere change can and will take you out of your comfort zone! You must go outside your comfort zone sometimes to experience the blessings of God. This is why changing your health will be a chore for some of you.

You will find yourself reprogramming your soul to make the necessary changes. Look at the changes for this woman again. She pours oil until she is out of pots and pans. She still has oil in that tiny jar, and he tells her to live off the rest.

As prophets, when we speak in agreement with what Father is saying, there is power released for the fulfillment of His plans. The Word from God will never fail (Luke 1:37). Now that we know that is true, why are we in such bad health?

Do we not believe it? Or do we fail to do it because we don't believe it?

Our tongue manifests the power of life and death, and those who love it will eat its fruit (Prov. 18:21). Prophet, do you want to be healthy? You know what you need to do. The reality is that you need a supernaturally charged atmosphere around you to function, and we need to function in establishing our health.

The anointing is something that can't be duplicated. It may be copied, but the anointing brings the authentic power of change. As prophets, let's strive for the supernatural atmosphere around us at all times.

Creating the right atmospheres and environments means creating an atmosphere conducive to God's movement. Anything that requires growth has to have a certain kind of atmosphere or environment to grow in a healthy way. Prophets understand this about atmospheres.

1. Seeds only grow in specific environments.

2. Some prophets are like children in the womb and only thrive in specific environments.

3. Some prophets are experiencing pain right now because they were raised in a different environment. God has given us the authority to change our environment. We are anointed to speak it.

God has given us the authority to hinder, enhance, create and shift our atmospheres and environment. We all are charged to play in creating the right atmosphere around us. For God to heal, move and set people free in our ministries, we have to create the right kind of environment.

God's love transforms the heart of God's prophets and qualifies them to become carriers of His glory. It is the love of God that has the power to transform a lost and dying world.

Every prophet should have a passion growing to see the saturated glory of God as people surrender their lives to Jesus. In today's society, this shift in thinking requires a different set of tools than previous generations. As prophets, we are compelled to seek revelation on making this a reality.

The primary ministry of the prophet is to focus on the activities of heaven and see heaven's supernatural reality released on earth. By establishing the Church in Christ and His love, they lay the proper foundation to cultivate the atmosphere of heaven that attracts God's presence.

Let me repeat this; this is the atmosphere where the gifts of the Spirit flow with miracles, signs, and wonders. This is the atmosphere of the supernatural.

I want to give you six ways a prophet can speak to change the atmosphere for supernatural miracles. My goal in this chapter of the book is to recognize the basics of a supernatural atmosphere and how you can benefit, especially your health and other areas of your life. You are not reading this book by mistake.

Prophet, do you need a miracle in your health or any area of your life? Pay special attention to these six ways which are the result of a healthy soul at work.

1. Focus And Talk About God's Agenda.

It is easy to focus on the difficulty and the pain in a trial or test. Prophets take a special kind of focus to comprehend the Spirit of God. This requires an intimate relationship with God. This will always give you a Kingdom perspective. For the purposes of God, this is how the atmosphere will shift.

2. Always Speak "Blessings."

Speaking, praying, or declaring words of blessing over people, situations, and over ourselves will change the atmosphere. As a prophet, you must understand that a blessing can be spoken normally. Prophets, your words are powerful and change the atmosphere. Prophets you can offer to pray a blessing over a person or situation incorporate blessing as an example in our family life. Words of blessing will change the atmosphere.

3. Prophets Pray with Prophetic Praise and a Spirit of Thanksgiving

We know that prophetic praise and prayer celebrate God's outcome before it even manifests physically. Our declarations of praise and thanks shift the atmosphere and contain the power needed: power for a breakthrough or a miracle. Prophets and seers, you must know that God's power is released when we pray according to His will in Jesus' name. Prophets, whose name are we praying in, and do we believe our prayers?

4. Use Prophetic Scripture Declaration

Seek God for specific prophetic scriptures that reflect His heart and purpose and what He is doing. The prophetic medium gives us insight from the Holy Spirit. We are to use God's Word to be God's intended outcome for a situation or people. There is the tremendous authority when we declare God's Word. Review Genesis chapter #1.

5. Prophets Should Take Every Opportunity to Share the Gospel

In John 6:63 Jesus said, "His words are full of the Spirit and life." Our goal must be to be more like Him. Prophets can speak life-giving words full of the Holy Spirit and empower God's purposes!

The anointing is for anyone that needs it. The level of anointing is available to all who are hungry for it. This includes young and old, extrovert and introvert, new and mature Christian. Prophets need to be given the opportunity to step out in the anointing.

6. We Must Demonstrate God's Love

Healing, deliverance, signs, and wonders are all extremely exhilarating in the prophetic ministry. Laying hands on someone and seeing them healed is a truly awesome experience.

Galatians 5:6 reminds us prophets that our faith works through God's love. Signs and wonders are needed to direct people toward the love of God. If we don't equip our people to ground their walk in love, healing becomes just another fad that's fun temporarily but with no lasting effect.

Jesus gives us an example of being around people who doubt or are too focused on the messenger instead of the message. The atmosphere will not change because of nonbelievers.

Mark 6:2-6 is the story of Jesus, the carpenter's son. The people were focused on Him more than they were on being healed. A prophet is not appreciated in their own town. Many of you know this being around your relatives in your hometown."

Now prophet you are prospering. Your words have created a supernatural atmosphere and you are in good health. Proclaim it now, whatever your health status is. While we do this, let us look at a known basic diet for a prophet of God.

CHAPTER 9

The Prophet's Diet

Prophet, lets establish an essential now generation diet. Let me confirm that this information in this chapter is not intended as medical advice, simply general known public knowledge.

Let us take what we learned about our souls in the previous chapters and apply it to our everyday lives. We start in earnest now as we discuss the prophet's diet. Yes, we are merely just sharing even more about our souls and health.

Think and consider it for yourself. Make sure you consult with your medical professionals and exercise your belief in God. This information is for the continued maturation of the prophet in their physical body.

Health is an interesting thing, and our souls make it that way. We have spent time learning that our soul is critical to our health, and that is a fact.

Prophets let us understand that some in our ranks may be unhealthy. Certain things are always harmful, like an enlarged heart, mutated blood cells, torn muscles, etc. Spiritually, some things are just as unhealthy also. Scripture lists hatred, lust, avarice, selfishness, and many others.

How do these things seek us through the soul? The Ten Commandments and other admonitions protect our health and the health of those around us.

Yes, prophet, there are spiritual variables just as there are physical. Let us understand that being healthy and better if they pray or serve is vital for some. Choose your diet wisely and know that it is best for you.

It is a full-time job to monitor my diet versus my cravings, which I like so much. Ultimately God, the great physician, will prescribe what each of us needs to provide the optimum spiritual and physical health. We discover these things as we dare to grow in our relationship with God. My prayer is that you see the importance of the soul in this process.

As a prophet or apostle, take your health seriously. It affects your ability to live well and serve others. We can look at the prophet Daniel's example. We now see that 21st century Christians are faced with a similar dilemma as he was in around 606 B.C.

He was forced to choose between Nebuchadnezzar's rich food and a vegetarian diet. Let us focus on Daniel, chapter one, where he rightly chose the latter. This scenario has come full circle in our now generation.

We have our standard everyday diet, or we can choose a healthy diet such as a vegetarian diet. Can you handle such a diet? Our soul affords us the opportunity to achieve the level of health that God intended for us since the creation. Learn how to be healthy in God's way!

A sample prophetic diet should be designed to cleanse the body of toxins and chemicals and input needed nutrients for maximum body operations. The prophet must watch what they eat. Your body is the temple of God. We must ask, "Can I afford to eat this today? Or have I put too much _____ into my body to be effective for God?"

The best beverage we can drink prophets is simply water. There are many benefits of drinking water. On a personal note, I know I do not drink enough water, but I will improve that. Public research has shown that water will aid in weight loss if we drink enough. Water is critical to all our bodily functions. Water helps burn our metabolism faster.

Drinking water is looked at to make the hunger sensations go away. I am learning to drink more water as I crave my favorite unhealthy foods and sweetened fluids.

Join me as I challenge you to drink more water. I like my tasty fluids as much as anyone, but the benefits of water are simply too much to list and way too apparent to us in this generation.

We all must take steps to control and watch the high amounts of sugar and fats in our diets. We have to protect our food consumption of processed and fast foods.

Our job is too important, and our bodies are critical to accomplishing the work God has given us. We have to get this right. We want the power of God to flow through us, and we need to be able to handle it.

We see specific biblical diets throughout scripture that work for various prophets. This was clearly about our relationship with God and what He wanted in our bodies for us to function at our optimum.

There are some great benefits of drinking more water than we usually do. Drinking water enhances our ability to lose fat. Studies show that water is essential to chemical reactions in the body.

We need to drink water for our kidneys and liver to function correctly. I was surprised to find out that water stops headaches and back pain in some cases. Even muscle spasms have been connected to not drinking enough water.

I am not a doctor, nor do I propose to be one, but the amount of shared knowledge available today as we seem to waste more and more time drinking our favorite fluids is staggering. The reality is that we need to drink more water.

We will look better, and we will feel better. There will be a difference when we monitor our diets. This is the only body we will get, and I encourage you to tackle your diet in the simplest ways, and it will pay off.

On a final note, we have talked about our health as prophets in the simplest forms. Again note that I am not a physician, and this is not medical advice.

Take your time and plan how to eat and what you need to drink to stay healthy. Numerous teas are suitable for the consumer depending on who you are and your body. There is a reality that we need to get to know ourselves better as we grow in God. I want to now share with you about another area of the health of a prophet and their soul. Let us talk about the Prophet's Red File now.

CHAPTER 10

The Prophet's Red File

Prophet, your life is essential to someone in your life besides you! Make sure you have the necessary documents available to you in an emergency. Remember that your soul is the laptop in your life, and it will process vital information.

The prophet's red file is vital to every prophet of relevance. We, the prophets, have spent far too much time working in ministry and have nothing to show when we are finally called home to Glory. I submit this chapter to you as a prophet with a healthy soul. This book has focused on the soul as it connects to the health of a prophet. This is a vital part of soul health.

My goal has been to make this connection real for each prophet who reads this book. This chapter is for every prophet who seeks to understand the total soul importance of their health and keep their soul in a place of peace as they do the work of God. This is priceless.

Let me mention again that I am not a physician, but I am concerned about my health just as I know you are about yours. The red file is the list of needed documents that will make your transition in any phase of life more accessible, including your leaving this world.

Many of you, like myself, have seen people leave this world. When this happens many times, we all know there is chaos because of poor preparation. The Prophets Red File will help this type transition in life and bring peace of mind, which is soul peace.

This list is not an all in all exclusive list, but one to handle your life as you will affect the lives of others. Every seer needs to establish and put together a personal prophetic Red File.

The Red File will act as the paper trail of your healthy soul. Here you will have copies of every important document needed and necessary to re-build your personal life and also, celebrate your life because you cared for others enough to pre-pare for God calling you home.

This file is essential for a spouse or family member in the face of any catastrophic or emer-gency event. This file includes financial and op-erational life in the aftermath of the chaos.

This list is a sample list of what you will need. Remember, you are a prophet to the nations, and even you could get sick or perhaps die, and your entire life needs to be healthy including your vi-tal paperwork.

This file is vital as an emergency arises, or you find that your access to your home and office is destroyed or not available.

This suggested list is a minimum of items you would want to include. Prophet, consider this list frequently and update it as needed depending on your situation.

Prophet, you will need to adjust this list to cover all aspects of your life.

Let me suggest the following list:

- Birth certificates for your family and yourself.
- A copy of everyone's Social Security Cards.
- Marriage certificate / Ministry certificates / Adoption papers (if applicable)
- Drivers licenses, Real ID's, and any trusted traveler products.
- Include the deed, mortgage documents, or any loan documents to your home or rental paperwork
- The copy of any car title or car paperwork you own or have registered.

• All your life and health insurance policies and any supporting paperwork including benefit cards.

• Copies of your current bank cards and or any credit cards.

• Inventory your valuable household items, and personal items at the office

• Photographic inventory of people in your house

• Your personal and or ministry Tax returns, at least three years

• All Wills and any power of attorney

• Important papers such as trusts if you have any beneficial interest

• Safe deposit boxes information

• Contact information for all key people in your life.

• Access to your banking information

• All documents that prove your ownership of private placements and alternative investments

• A current list of User IDs and Passwords for access to all electronic-based information formats

• A complete list of assets and liabilities, with a footnote for each item

My most sincere blessings to you; let's stay healthy as we run this race. We all have much work to do. Let me know if I can help or assist you in any way. God Bless you, my friend, and thank you for reading this book! I appreciate you.

About The Author

Apostle Ken Cox started serving God in 1994 after a series of unforeseen life failures. Out of the military and seemly starting life over again, by 2000, Apostle Cox had found his life calling as a Prophet. The challenge of learning and understanding presented a new frontier. Apostle Cox dove into the process and has now emerged as a well-traveled prophet who serves the Body of Christ as an Apostle.

Apostle Cox, along with his wife, Prophetess Sabina Cox are the leaders of Where Eagles Fly Fellowship Inc., a fellowship of prophets and apostle across the USA and beyond who are dedicated and focused on establishing the prophetic gift back into society as they raise up prophets around the country and abroad.

Apostle Cox and Prophetess Cox are available for Revivals, Conferences and Meetings. They have been featured in meetings and sought-after to teach and instruct the prophetic for ministries seeking to learn more about the gift. Apostle and Prophetess Cox have 3 children and 4 grandkids as of this writing and currently reside in Durham, NC. Contact them through the Where Eagles Fly office at 919-695-3375 or 919-213-1328 or at www.whereeaglesfly.us.

Index

A

B

I

P